An Elephant in the House

An elephant came
to our house.
It sat on the living room
floor and watched TV.

"What's that elephant
doing in here?"
asked Dad.

"It's watching
the news and
the weather report,"
Mum replied.

"It's too big.
It's got to go," said Dad.

"I've tried to shoo it away," said Mum. "It won't go."

"All right then.
Help me push it out," said Dad.

So Mum and Dad pushed the elephant as hard as they could.

But the elephant didn't
move an eyelid.
It didn't move
a hair on its tail.

Along came Grandma and Grandpa.
"Who let that enormous elephant in?" asked Grandpa.

"It came in all by itself," said Dad.

"Why don't you chase it out?" asked Grandpa.

"Why don't *you* chase it out?" asked Grandma.

So Grandpa yelled at the elephant, "Shoo, you big, enormous thing!"

But the elephant stayed where it was.

"I know what we'll do," said Grandpa.
"We'll push it out."

"We've already tried that," said Mum.

"Not with us, you haven't," said Grandpa.
"I'm very good at pushing elephants."

So Mum, Dad, Grandma, and Grandpa pushed the huge elephant until they were blue in the face.

But the elephant still didn't move.

Along came John.
"What are you doing?"
he asked.

"We're trying to get rid of this elephant," said Mum.

"We've pushed and pulled," said Dad.

"We've pulled and pushed," said Grandma.

"We've got no more push left,"
said Grandpa.

"That's not the way to get rid of an elephant," said John.

John took a flower
from a vase and tickled
one of the elephant's feet.
The elephant snorted.
The elephant wiggled.
Its tail twitched.
It pretended it was
still watching the news
and the weather report.

John tickled the second foot.
The elephant flapped its ears.

John tickled the third foot.
Tears came out
of the elephant's eyes.
But it still pretended
to watch TV.

When John tickled the fourth
foot, it was too much
for the elephant.

It rolled over on its back.
It shook all over.
It laughed so loudly
that the window cracked.

John held the flower
to the elephant's trunk.
"Do you want some more?"
he asked. But he didn't have
to ask a second time.

The elephant got to its feet
and ran out of the house.
It ran bellowing
down the road.

"That's how you get rid of an elephant," said John.

"It's good we had some flowers," said Grandpa.